Dave's LIFE LINES

Written and Collected By
Dave Willert

Illustrated by Doug Kuhl

"Dave's LIFE LINES," written and collected by Dave Willert.
ISBN 978-1-949756-90-6 (softcover).

Published 2019 by Virtualbookworm.com Publishing Inc., P.O. Box 9949, College Station, TX 77842, US. ©2019, Dave Willert.

All rights reserved. No part of this publication may be reproduced, stored in a retrieval system, or transmitted in any form or by any means, electronic, mechanical, recording or otherwise, without the prior written permission of Dave Willert.

DEDICATION

This book is dedicated to my loving wife, Margaret, who has always been a major supporter of my creative endeavors, as well as a continuous source of inspiration. I want to especially thank her for suggesting the title for this book, which just like her... I believe to be perfect! I would also like to dedicate this book to my son, Alex, whom I am thoroughly proud of, not only for his many achievements, but also for the wonderful person he has become, along with his amazing wife, Katie. In addition, I would like to dedicate this book to my very good friend, Doug Kuhl, who has always been like part of the family and is the first one there, when any of us is in need. (Like my need for someone to do this book's illustrations.) Additionally, I would like to thank my mother, Ruth, who passed away in 2018, at the age of 96, but left behind a shining legacy. She encouraged each of her ten children, to never become "worry-warts," but to think positively instead, and have faith that things will always work out well in the end. Finally, let me thank all of my former teachers in school, oh so many years ago. I didn't know it then, but many of them prepared me for life, not only through the subjects they taught... but through their encouragement, caring, sage advice, patience and second chances.

Life is meant to be a wonderful blessing for every one of us, however, our individual definitions of a 'blessed life,' can be very different from one another. So, with that in mind, I want to thank everyone I know or have ever known, for giving me such an interesting and diverse collection of experiences and conversations to base many of these motivational thoughts on. In

Dave's LIFE LINES

this way, we all wrote this book together. Thank you for the inspiration. May God continue to bless each of us, according to our needs, every day of our lives!

Sincerely,
Dave Willert

TABLE OF CONTENTS

INTRODUCTION vi
Chapter One: A POSITIVE ATTITUDE! 1
Chapter Two: HELPING YOURSELF! 28
Chapter Three: LOVE & FRIENDSHIP! 65
Chapter Four: ACHIEVEMENT! 94
Chapter Five: RANDOM THOUGHTS! 127
Illustrations 181

INTRODUCTION

This book, *Dave's Life Lines*, certainly has a curious title. The implication being that I have written a book about "saving people" from drowning by throwing them a *lifeline*... which is not exactly the case. In reality, however, that reasoning is not too far from the truth. *Dave's Life Lines* is a simple self-help book containing 588 *motivational thoughts and life observations* that I have either been inspired to 'jot down' over the years, or glean from other very worthy sources. I'm sure I will read or continue to come up with additional 'thoughts,' long after this book has been published... but this is, at least, a healthy start! Many authors have compiled books of this sort. The first I ever read was Benjamin Franklin's *Sir Richard's Almanac,* which was a wild success, published in the American colonies during the eighteenth century, for some 26 years. Mark Twain was also a master at writing motivational and humorous sayings. If any of my motivational sayings (or maxims, as they are also called) should sound similar to a few of theirs, I apologize... but I am not shy in telling you that both Benjamin Franklin and Mark Twain, wrote wonderful and often humorous maxims, which are still a great source of inspiration and humor to their readers today. I am actually very proud to have my work inspired by theirs! I sincerely hope that you will find some of the thoughts included in this book, to be both useful and thought provoking, as you continue setting a course through your own life.

This book is relatively short and easy to read, and I'm hoping there is something in it that will truly catch your interest. By no means do I claim to be a "professional deep thinker," but I do

A Positive Attitude!

stand behind all of the writings I have shared in this book. I must, however, warn you that I thrive in the dimension *of happy*, so a lot of these thoughts are steered toward that very outcome! I do not expect all of these thoughts to be meaningful to everyone who reads *Dave's Life Lines*, however... but if any of them should give you just a wee bit of illumination, then for me, this book was well worth writing.

My family and friends encouraged me to write this book to share some of the *motivational thoughts* I have posted on Facebook, over the past ten years. Each of those offerings was originally posted because they were special to me at the time and I hoped they might also hold some universal appeal. Some of these thoughts were developed during my younger years, inspired by my friends, parents, teachers and nine siblings, while others transpired more recently, inspired by members of my immediate family and friends, my forty years of teaching, miscellaneous events and even a random thought I may have had from time to time. In addition, as I mentioned earlier, there are a select number of 'special quotes,' which I borrowed from other writers and personalities (whom I clearly give credit to in this book), because I was so moved by what they said and how they said it. My heartfelt thanks, in no particular order, goes out to the following 65 people: **Norman Vincent Peale, Carl Sandberg, Thomas Edison, Frederich Niedzsche, Dr. Seuss, Buddha, Anthony Robbins, Dante, Fred Rogers, A. A. Milne, Robert A. Heinlein, Fritz Leiber, Kurt Vonnegut, Charles Dickens, Edgar Allan Poe, Ayn Rand, Theodore Roosevelt, Gloria Steinem, George Eliot, Oscar Wilde, Quentin Crisp, James F. Byrnes, Reba McEntire, Sir Arthur Conan Doyle, Elbert Hubbard, Lucius Annaeus Seneca, R. Buckminister Fuller, Roald Dahl, Benjamin Franklin, Auguste Rodin, Victor Hugo, Robert Frost, Vince Lombardi, Leonardo da Vinci, Samuel Johnson, James Thurber, Lewis Carroll, Michelangelo, Charles Chaplin, Ray Bradbury, Jimmy Dean, Ralph Waldo Emerson, George Bernard Shaw, Lao Tzu, Mother Teresa, Bertrand de Jouvenel, Fred Astaire, John A Shedd, Albert Einstein, George Addair, Socrates, C. S. Lewis, Charles Lamb, Helen Keller, Aesop,**

Dave's LIFE LINES

Doug Kuhl, Abraham Lincoln, Joseph F. Newman, Robert Louis Stevenson, Bernard Meltzer, Mahatma Gandhi, St. Francis of Assisi, Mark Twain, Dalai Lama and Rodney Dangerfield, for providing the 82 brilliant thoughts, which I have gladly and appreciatively made part of this book. To my thinking, a motivational book is best when a number of very different minds have directly or indirectly collaborated on it, giving the reader the greatest chance of connecting. Surprisingly, I found that all of the thoughts I composed or collected, basically fell into five categories:

A POSITIVE ATTITUDE

HELPING YOURSELF

LOVE & FRIENDSHIP

ACHIEVEMENT

RANDOM THOUGHTS

So, I made those the five distinct chapters of this book! Over the years, I actually posted other topics on Facebook, that fell into the categories of **RELIGION, POLITICS** and **SPORTS**, but these subjects can be contentious. So, being the diplomat I am, rather than taking the chance of offending anyone, I opted to leave those *dangerous* chapters out of the book. Remember, I like to live in the dimension of happy!

One last caveat… to be honest, although I didn't intentionally plagiarize anyone else's work, I am not positive that all of my own 'motivational thoughts,' are actually completely original, and unbeknownst to me, were not written and published previously by other writers. You may have even personally come up with some of these thoughts, yourself, while in a 'motivational' mood. For these reasons, I don't claim to be the only person to have ever thought up or written down these maxims… only the first person to have ever published them in this unique collection. I hope you enjoy them. Happy reading!

Chapter One:
A POSITIVE ATTITUDE!

There may be nothing so invaluable in preparing a person for the unexpected twists and turns they will undoubtedly encounter as they travel through life, than a sincere ***positive attitude***. There are so many different ways of expressing a positive attitude, but mostly, you will see it demonstrated through words or deeds. But no matter what... a positive attitude can never be hidden! It's that honest little smile on a person's face every time you see them or you may sense their natural inclination to always be kind and helpful toward others. Sometimes, having a positive attitude doesn't appear to fit-in amongst people who spend most of their time complaining about everyone and everything in sight. But I believe this thought to be a fallacy. In reality, I believe that all of those stressed-out and overworked people may simply need a good hug to join the club! Bad situations sometimes cause people to temporarily lose their positivity and to begin thinking and acting negatively. But no one could be happy acting like that forever, could they? I believe that a person in a foul mood is a person just waiting to have a reason to feel positive... and as I mentioned... to experience a great big hug!

When you find yourself not feeling very positive, yourself, perhaps some of these motivational thoughts will help you to find your way back? After all, that is the reason they were created.

Dave's LIFE LINES

"If you are loved, doing what you want to do and adequately handling all of those unexpected dramas... don't you think that life is kind of fun?"

"The greatest compliment a person can give you... is their personal respect."

"It's easy to dwell on what is going wrong in your life, but it's much more fun to find a bit of happiness in every situation."

"Money is at its best when it is used to benefit others."

"My definition of a wasted day is one without a worthy purpose. My definition of a <u>wasted life</u>… is that, times the number of days we are alive!"

"I always imagine that I am a young, talented, good looking person… until I look into the mirror… And then I KNOW I am!"

"Be sure you are evaluating your successes exclusively through the lenses which you deem to be most important. Pay little attention to the usual, 'fame and fortune,' if they really don't apply."

"Rudeness may be forgiven and in time, mostly forgotten… but the memory of kindness…never fades."

Dave's LIFE LINES

"Be creative and a self-starter! On any given day, it is far easier to create an exciting adventure for yourself, than to wait for one to conveniently fall into your lap out of nowhere."

"Taking a risk is like shopping for a new car. You never really know what you've got until after you've taken that first test drive."

"Feeling good about our days, begins and ends with how we fill them up."

"Sometimes the best decisions are not necessarily the most popular ones, or the easiest."

"Never make assumptions, no matter what people tell you. An unbiased person holds out for any and all possibilities… until they personally find what they believe to be the definitive answer."

"Life is full of wonderful people… who sometimes disagree."

"Just because something is the way it is… does not necessarily make it right."

Dave's LIFE LINES

"I believe in Santa Claus, no matter how many people disagree. To be precise, he lives 365 days a year (366 in leap years) in our hearts… and he takes a world 'gifting' tour every Christmas Eve!"

"For where your treasure is, your heart will be there also."
(Matthew 6:21)

"There are many wonderful things happening in our lives everyday... If we only open our eyes to see them!"

"In life, each of us is like a beautifully wrapped gift, being opened... slowly and patiently. And guess what? The best is always yet to come!"

"Sometimes our dreams make better sense than the reality that we are living in."

"Pizzazz is the perfect alignment of focus and determination!"

"Truth paints a perfection in vibrant colors… that lying, can only poorly imitate!"

"Happy memories are like diamonds. Yes, they are beautiful, but more importantly… They are unbreakable."

"If God had wanted all people to think and act in the exact same way… he would not have given us free will or the ability to change our minds!"

*"On a particularly bad day,
I close my eyes and clear my mind
of all the anxieties that I have
accumulated. When I finally open
them up again, and only then, do I
see the goodness and the beauty of
the world shining through…
once again!"*

*"When you are truly a positive
person, you never feel the need to
criticize others… in order to
build yourself up."*

*"Every time I am
asked who has inspired me the most,
my truthful response is, "On which
day?"*

Dave's LIFE LINES

"Those with the most vivid imaginations are capable of creating sheer magic!"

◈◈◈

"Success finds a way... Failure finds an excuse!"

◈◈◈

"Everything you have ever wanted is on the other side of fear."
(George Addair)

◈◈◈

"The secret of change is to focus all of your energy, not on fighting the old... but on building the new."
(Socrates)

◈◈◈

"Kindness magically makes any situation happier!"

"Creativity is intelligence having fun."
(Albert Einstein)

Dave's LIFE LINES

*"When you have children,
being their parent never ends...
Thank goodness!"*

*"Every great achievement
began as a great idea."*

*"Beauty varies by interpretation...
Integrity does not."*

*"Our true purpose in life...
is often discovered by accident."*

*"Look forward to every day you live...
and you will never be bored."*

"If someone asked me, today, what my greatest personal achievement was throughout my entire lifetime, I would have to say... 'I don't know. I'm not through yet.'"

"Regardless of how difficult things were yesterday, today must begin with a clean slate."

"Being happy means that it's okay if what you do in life does not seem awesome to anybody else... just as long as it does to you."

"Commit to 'happiness' every day of your life!"

Dave's LIFE LINES

"A positive person, patiently goes about getting things done, while a cynical person, gloats, and says, 'I told you so,' every time things don't go exactly as planned!"

"Each of us becomes a truly enlightened person, once we realize that our personal adventure through life, no matter how meaningful… is not the only one that matters."

"Make whatever you do every day… well worth remembering."

"A grudge is a self-inflicted pain that never stops hurting and can only be healed… from the heart."

"Nothing warms the heart so much as witnessing a dynamic and positive change in someone you care about."

"Especially when experiencing serious problems, it is so imperative to remember... how truly wonderful it is to be alive!"

"Helping others is the easiest way to find meaning in your life."

"Where there is doubt, there is self-inflicted failure. Where there is confidence... there is hope."

"If we were all meant to be the center of attention… there would be no one left to adore us!"

"Focusing too much on the negative, even for a little while, has the power to rob us of what should be our natural inclination to be positive thinkers!"

"Finding our proper places in the world, is not always easy. Ultimately, we may need to create them ourselves."

"I mostly remember people, not for how talented or smart they are… but how thoughtful and kind!"

"People who freely and happily do kind things for others… are my favorite kind of role models."

"Let every deed, every word and every thought show the best in you… because that is how people should know you."

"Positive people are our best defense against hopelessness."

"When you do something from the heart, you don't need others to verify its worth!"

"I am the wisest man alive, for I know one thing, and that is that I know nothing." (Socrates)

"You know that you are happy when you look forward to waking-up each morning and sad that there aren't more hours in the day."

*"Hope is not always reasonable…
but that doesn't make it any less real."*

*"When I let go of what I am,
I become what I might be."
(Lao Tzu)*

*"It is not only possessing a positive
attitude that makes a person an
optimist… but equally important is
their lack of a negative one."*

*"Words can sometimes be dishonest
or hollow. In truth, you generally
know a person better through
their actions."*

Dave's LIFE LINES

"The excitement of a purposeful new beginning should always trump the uncertainty of change."

"To the artist, there is never anything ugly in nature." (Auguste Rodin)

"We cannot control everything that happens to us, but we can control how we deal with it… negatively or positively."

"Assuming that everyone has something good about them, and then focusing on that… is far healthier than hating the world."

Helping Yourself!

"Those who don't believe in magic… will never find it!" (Roald Dahl)

Dave's LIFE LINES

"A positive attitude will encourage your friends and annoy your enemies. What's not to like?"

"An effective leader inspires by positive example, while simultaneously attempting to pull the very best out of everyone."

"Life is not only meant to be tolerated… It is meant to be enjoyed!"

*"True happiness is…
to enjoy the present without anxious dependence upon the future."
(Lucius Annaeus Seneca)*

*"Someone who spends their life
tearing down people and things...
will never know the joys of
being a positive person."*

*"Seeing a glass as only half full,
doesn't take into account the other
50% of potential, which will lead to
making the glass completely full...
once we figure-out a way to fill it up."*

*"Positive thoughts lead to positive
actions, which of course...
lead to happiness!"*

*"Telling the truth,
never goes out of style."*

Dave's LIFE LINES

*"When you think positively, every day will bring you a plethora of positive adventures! Even your adventures that aren't so positive, won't seem nearly as bad as they could… because naturally…
you put a positive spin on them!"*

"Being a good person, according to most definitions, has little to do with fitting in with other people around you. You want to fit in, of course… but sometimes it's just a matter of choosing your beliefs over your popularity."

"Nothing we create is ever as great as its potential!"

"Sometimes we may consider ourselves unlucky, due to the twists and turns of our lives. But, maybe we just aren't interpreting things correctly? Maybe we are actually among the luckiest people on Earth?"

"Never give an opinion the same respect as you would give to a fact!"

"Unfortunately, being a positive person does not guarantee that everyone will always get along with you. However, that shouldn't stop you from still trying to get along with THEM."

Dave's LIFE LINES

"When we consider everything we do, everyone we meet and everything that spontaneously happens to us as somehow being positive and special, it makes it very difficult for us to find fault with our lives or at least to complain too loudly. In its very subtle way, a positive attitude gently sets us on a course... to happiness."

"Be yourself. Although that may not mean you'll be the richest and most popular person around... who cares... you'll be happier!"

"Anything is possible with a little imagination and a positive mindset."

"Learn from everything that happens. Even experiencing all of those tough times in life, somehow makes us stronger people, who are better prepared to handle similar surprises in the future... and to help others, to do the same."

"If positive people weren't around, there would be no one left to drive the cynics and pessimists crazy!"

Chapter Two:
HELPING YOURSELF!

The term, *'helping yourself'* is not nearly as obvious as it appears. We all learn throughout our lives to 'help ourselves' in a variety of ways, including the practical things like personal hygiene, getting dressed in the morning, learning to accept responsibility and hopefully learning how to get and keep a job and to balance a checkbook. But these skills are not enough to make most of us happy. How do we deal with stress, for example, or what keeps us from working our hardest at everything we do? In learning to personally improve, experience helps (both good and bad), as well as wise counsel. Hopefully, 'wise counsel,' is exactly what you will get from reading these motivational thoughts. You be the judge.

"When you possess an exceptional gift or talent, and your life ends prematurely, your greatest regret might be that you never 'found the time' in your life… to take advantage of it?"

"Stress is an unnecessary side effect of frustration which ravages the body and mind. Why not learn to live without it?"

"Actually believing that you are in many ways, the master of your own life... is required to make it so!"

"Hoping is good... but doing, is better."

"Look for the humor in each day... and then laugh out loud!"

"Ignore the naysayers! It is very important for us to feel proud of our own achievements. It is not being stuck-up... it's adding to our confidence!"

"If what you do doesn't matter to you, then it's hard to believe that it will matter to anyone else, either!"

"Being yourself and holding firm to your core values won't necessarily make you popular... but it will sure make you honest!"

"We can overcome losing just about everything we possess... except our hope!"

Helping Yourself!

"Whenever you feel a strong desire to do something creative, that's your heart calling! What more do you need to get started?"

"It doesn't matter how young or old you are, or your personal situation. A day is only 24 hours long for everyone. Don't waste any of it!"

"You will always feel better about your decisions… once you dare to make them for yourself!"

"One of the most effective ways to learn is through your own successes and failures."

Dave's LIFE LINES

"Taking responsibility for yourself and your future, sets-up your best chance of reaching your dreams."

∽∾∽∾

"A person's life is never without problems. However, dealing with them is the best way to gain wisdom - whether you win or you lose."

∽∾∽∾

"Our happiness is not dependent upon what we have been given in this life… but rather, by what we DO with it."

∽∾∽∾

"Integrity without knowledge is weak and useless, while knowledge without integrity is dangerous and dreadful." (Samuel Johnson)

"Everything we think, do and say becomes the story of our lives. If we want a more satisfying story to remember… then we had just better rewrite our futures differently!"

"Great skills don't happen overnight. A little practice every day, will go a long way."

"Life isn't about finding yourself. Life is about creating yourself." (George Bernard Shaw)

"Never stop running the race, no matter how far behind you may find yourself, at the moment."

Dave's LIFE LINES

"Happy memories are always there to pick us up on tough days, by reminding us how to smile and laugh."

"If you don't find hope and opportunity within reach of your life every morning… then you probably aren't looking hard enough!"

"On all matters, don't follow the crowd… Follow your heart."

"Make sure that if you are always busy… you are busy doing those things that you want to be doing."

"When you try hard to be a good person, but feel useless or invisible in the world, just remember that you ARE important. You are probably inspiring a number of people every day through your good attitude and actions. Just because they don't tell you that… doesn't mean it's not happening."

"True learning always involves alert and active participation."

"Try not to be consumed by all of the hatred in the world, just because that's what you see on the news. Life is also full of wonderful people, love and hope… and it's often much closer than you think!"

Dave's LIFE LINES

"Sometimes the key to a happier life is not changing yourself… but rather just putting more effort into BEING yourself."

"Whenever you are feeling overcome with stress, stop what you are doing and relax. Dare to be ordinary for a while."

*"You can outdistance that which
is running after you, but not
what is running inside you."
(Rwandan proverb)*

*"Who you were yesterday or who you
are today, does not need to be the
person you are tomorrow, if you have
the strength and inclination…
to make a change."*

*"As an adult, never allow others to
make important life decisions for
you, without your participation.
If you do, it may place you on a
direct path to regret."*

"It's never too late to be happy."

"He who appreciates what he has, has little need to miss what he doesn't."

"The majority of how good you feel about your day hinges upon your attitude. It's your ability to find that silver lining in an unpleasant situation… that points you out as being a positive person!"

"While others may laugh at them, always hold tight to your dreams, even if they seem ridiculous! Your dreams define you like nothing else."

"Take what you have and excel with it!"

"Pay attention to what's going on around you… or you might miss something very important!"

"Our talents and attitudes are our paintbrushes, and time our easel. It is completely up to us, how we decide to navigate our lives… and ultimately paint our life's portrait."

"Talking a good game is easy. But, go on to the next step if you are sincere about what you are saying. Learn to be a doer!"

"No matter what it is we do well, we can and should… always try to do it better."

"I tried, I failed, I moved on!"
(Anon)

"During the darkest times in our lives, we must never give up, but persevere until we find the light."

"Character cannot be developed in ease and quiet. Only through experience of trial and suffering can the soul be strengthened, ambition inspired, and success achieved."
(Helen Keller)

"Your personal character is formed by what you DON'T do, as much as by what you do."

"There is no wisdom gained from an experience, unless you choose to understand and to value it."

"Never allow the naysayers to silence you, even if it seems as if no one else agrees with you. If what you believe is honest and not dangerous toward anyone else, then you have every right to express yourself."

"Hardships often prepare ordinary people for an extraordinary destiny."
(C. S. Lewis)

"Your own positive mindset has the power to turn a completely dismal day into a hopeful one!"

"Growing up is a lifelong endeavor."

"Arrogance is just another form of blindness with your eyes open." (Albert Einstein)

"The world is simultaneously beautiful and ugly. It's up to us, individually, to determine which part we will spend our lives contributing to."

"None of us really knows what awaits us in the future, but it's a whole lot more fun to look forward to it... than to dread it!"

Helping Yourself!

"Self-reflection not only reveals who you are, but also... who you are not!"

"Learn to stand out from the crowd. Be thoughtful and kind!"

Dave's LIFE LINES

"It's nice to experience a magical moment… but it's even more satisfying to play a part in making one."

✦

"Never compete, as if you have already won. Someone, usually unexpectedly, is always inspired to beat you!"

✦

"You are making memories right now, but are they truly the memories… you want?"

✦

"No one can make you feel worthless, unless you already agree with them."

"Choose wisely! For every major decision you make today, there may be many years of consequences... both good and bad."

"Don't depend on others to determine what is most important to you... and what is not."

"Remember, we are not the center of the universe. It only feels that way when we are at our happiest."

"When you care deeply about a subject... Don't just learn it... Master it!"

"It's always lonely at the top. Being the best, begins and ends with you alone."

"Finding Fault with others does nothing to make you a better person."

"The person who works hard, only to please others, will never be as accomplished as the person who works hard to also please themselves… through always giving their best and striving to improve!"

"I have a plan. I am who I am! I don't need your approval… but I would love to talk about it."

"Learn to keep your emotions under control. Losing your cool may momentarily alleviate your stress... But at what cost?"

"Everyone is a bit of a pessimist, an optimist, a comedian and a drama queen. But the one you inhabit most... will surely define you."

"When you find something is seriously wrong with your life, doing nothing about it to improve your situation... is the same as accepting it."

"Never forget who you really are!"

"Technically, you are never too old to begin a new endeavor. It's all up to you! But heed this. Once you genuinely 'consider yourself too old'… you probably are!"

"A motivated person never stops learning, while a lazy person never chooses to begin!"

"Worry is like a rocking chair. It will give you something to do, but it won't get you anywhere." (Anon)

"Sometimes, something we thought was very important to us… as it turns out… isn't!"

"If I'm not exhausted by the end of the day... I'm probably not working hard enough."

"Neglecting your natural talents is like acting ungrateful to a friend who just gave you a gift, or purposely tearing up a check for a million dollars!"

"A little spontaneity each day, will keep your life pleasantly unpredictable."

"A nimble brain is like a genie, who has agreed to grant you all of your wishes... through your imagination."

"If you must have a flaw, let it be in your fashion sense, not in your character." (Anon)

"Be careful of letting your own expectations bleed through to what you expect from your children or friends. When it comes right down to it… everyone has the right to reach their own conclusions."

"Don't wish your life away when things don't seem to be going well. Beautiful things, people and experiences often seem to magically appear… in the wake of hard times."

Helping Yourself!

"There is no outside cure for exhibiting a lack of effort."

"When you find that your life is going in the wrong direction, don't forget… You can always choose to turn around."

"Living selfishly… always leads to a lonely end!"

"It's amazing to realize that sometimes by simply gaining a better self-image and a little confidence, we don't fear life anymore… We embrace it!"

"Every morning when we awake, we receive the amazing gift of life. But don't take any part of it for granted. Live each moment, full of enthusiasm and love, as if it were your last day on Earth… because no one really knows when that day will come."

"You are never too old to be what you might have been." (George Eliot)

"One day Alice came to a fork in the road and saw a Cheshire cat in a tree. 'Which road do I take?' she asked. 'Where do you want to go?' was his response. 'I don't know,' Alice answered. 'Then,' said the cat, 'it doesn't matter.'" (Lewis Carroll)

"When you're tired, no matter how busy you are... find the time to 'sneak' a little nap."

"It's a big waste of time and effort to create space in your life to 'hate' somebody... so why not let that story line die? Move ahead to other relationships and better story lines... and make your life joyful!"

"Begin each day with a happy thought and a smile."

Dave's LIFE LINES

"Happiness is not the recipe for making you into a positive thinker... It's the end result."

"Don't dwell on a sad or disappointing experience and don't gloat over a happy one. Just accept whatever it was and move forward, with an open mind, toward your life's next great possibility."

"Moving forward often involves going back... and fixing things first."

"I can resist everything... except temptation!"
(Oscar Wilde)

"Never hate a person for something they have said or done, if you are more understanding of that same offense when it involves your friends, family or even yourself. Offer equal understanding to everyone, and hopefully, when the time comes... you will receive the same courtesy from them."

"With self-discipline, most anything is possible." (Theodore Roosevelt)

"Do what you are inspired to do, to the best of your ability! Not for praise... but for satisfaction."

"Don't always depend on others to solve your problems. Sometimes, it's YOU, who has the best solutions!"

Dave's LIFE LINES

"The arts are not usually a way to make a living. They are a very human way of making life more bearable. Practicing an art, no matter how well or badly, is a way to make your soul grow, for heaven's sake!"
(Kurt Vonnegut)

"Free thinking combined with responsibility, beats 'no thinking' combined with forced indoctrination, any day!"

"WHAT you do is seldom more than a small part of WHO you are. Investigate, discover and take time to develop all of you."

"No matter what you believe, there is always somebody, somewhere... who is bound to agree with you!"

"Freedom feels so natural. In fact, you generally don't even start thinking about it... until it starts being eroded away from you."

"Always know the difference between doing something to 'help' a person, regardless of their gratitude... and doing something to 'please' a person... because of their gratitude."

"At first glance, a tree in the forest might look big and strong, while in truth, it's actually dying from root rot... Never trust first glances."

"Beware. A leader, by definition, is simply someone who 'leads' others. But a 'leader' who follows their own agenda instead of listening to all of their constituents, is not a leader at all… they are just another thinly veiled, self-centered, narcissist!"

Helping Yourself!

"Be careful to practice doing things over and over again, in EXACTLY the right way. This will guarantee that you learn them correctly. Remember, 'Practice Makes Permanent!'"
(Doug Kuhl)

"No amount of lying will change who you are."

Dave's LIFE LINES

"There comes a time in each of our lives, when all that we really need... is a great big hug!"

"Never allow anyone who has no faith in your abilities, to act as the final word in determining whether or not you should attempt something you really want to attempt... and feel very qualified to undertake!"

"A good decision doesn't need to take a long time to reach... it only needs to "feel" right."

"Being upset is never a good excuse for acting rudely."

"Everyone has the power to create their own happiness through focusing on positive and encouraging thoughts and then acting on them... while simultaneously chasing away the dark mood or apathy they replace."

"Inspiration never tells you when it's coming... but when it does, it might behoove you to invite it in."

"Make sure that if you are always busy, you are busy doing those things that you <u>want</u> to be doing."

"An unlimited supply of explanations along with the transferring of fault... won't fix a bad decision."

Dave's LIFE LINES

"Avoid people whose entire existence seems to be to persuade you, usually against your will, to buy, join or do something, which they directly benefit from. They are the piranhas that give sales people a bad name."

"Keep alert. Every day of our lives represents the challenge of overcoming obstacles... which are not always obvious."

"If you do everything for profit, then profit is your ultimate reward. But if you do everything out of love…"

"If you don't have an exciting long-term goal in your life to dream about in your spare time... You don't know what you are missing!"

"Change doesn't always make things better or worse... only different."

"In life, it's not really your responsibility to understand why some people, regardless of your efforts, are just so difficult to work with. On the other hand, it often IS your responsibility to keep moving forward... in spite of them."

"We are never completely alone... as long as we have our memories."

"Don't waste a moment worrying about death. Always focus on living and all of the wonderful things you can do to fill up your days... You'll have a much better time."

"The trouble with most of us is that we would rather be ruined with praise than saved by criticism." (Norman Vincent Peale)

"Everyone has made mistakes, in the past, which they continue to feel badly for. If you are truly sorry, why do you continue suffering? Why not apologize to those you may have hurt, forgive yourself... and embrace a fresh start?"

Chapter Three:
LOVE & FRIENDSHIP!

Love and friendship are such integral parts of each of our lives. Can you imagine going through life without a single person to trust in, talk to or mutually care for? Both love & friendship must be nurtured, and never taken for granted. The following motivational thoughts don't deal with love & friendship as merely passing phases, but as a more serious social situation. A good friendship always has the potential to blossom into *lifelong* friendship or even love, if all parties feel so inclined. Life is so much more meaningful because of both! Enjoy!

"Never underestimate the lifelong value of love."

"Kindness ought to be more than an occasional nicety. It should be a way of life."

"Being a great conversationalist lies more in knowing what interests your fellow conversers have… and less in simply sharing your opinions."

"The best things about a happy friendship are not only the unforgettable memories you gain, but the excitement of knowing… there will be plenty more!"

"Value every great friendship as if it will last a lifetime… and then maybe it will?"

"Make today special for both you and your loved ones."

"A great friendship is like a great memory. No matter how much time has passed since we last visited it... it never ceases to be special to us."

"If you truly care about others... they are much more likely to care about you."

"As a rule, do what you say you will do, even when it's inconvenient... and you will become a person, who others can trust!"

"If you should ever find yourself in a one-sided friendship? I'm sorry... that is not a friendship!"

"In the spirit of compromise, I find embracing the idea that, 'everyone who does not see things in the very same way that I do, is not necessarily wrong'… greatly increases my circle of friends."

"Like our cars, computers, televisions, phones and other high tech devices in our lives, it's easy to take our friends and family for granted. Don't forget to greet them with a kind word and a sincere smile, every time you see them!"

"Love is the condition in which the happiness of another person, is essential to your own."
(Robert A. Heinlein)

"The wonderful thing about doing something nice for someone is that it not only feels great to both the recipient and the giver, but also to everyone who observes it or hears about it afterward. A good deed is truly the gift that keeps on giving!"

"To more honestly get to know somebody, look first at what they are... instead of what they are not."

"Do I not destroy my enemies when I make them my friends?"
(Abraham Lincoln)

"Helping others doesn't need any further reward."

"People are lonely because they build walls, instead of bridges."
(Joseph F. Newman)

"Friendship is born out of people finding things in common and wanting to spend more time together. It may even grow into caring for one another and if cultivated correctly, there is no limit to the growth of the relationship... and no expiration."

"Some people will always be toxic toward you, no matter what you do or say. It's their choice, for whatever the reason. For your own peace of mind, hold no grudge against them... and move on."

Love & Friendship

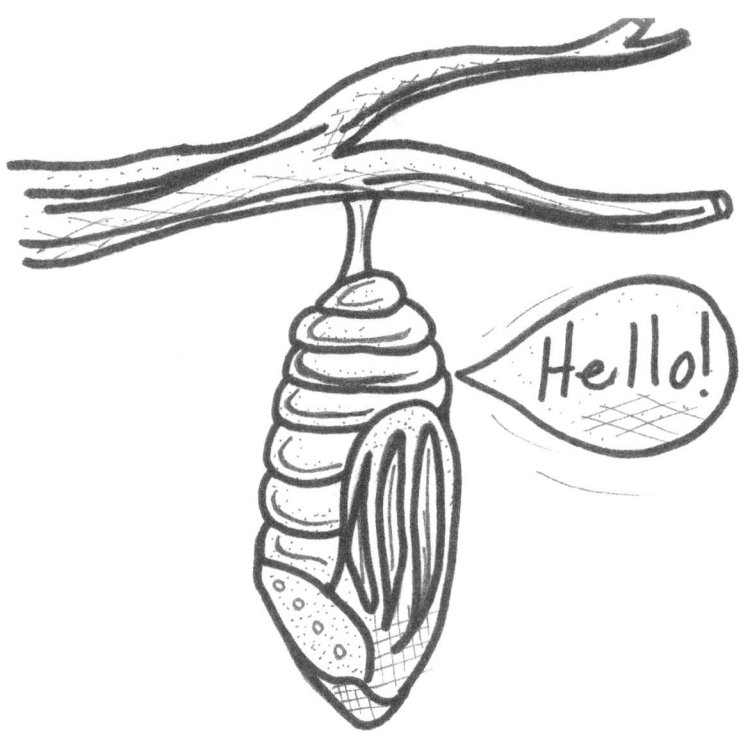

"Until you begin sharing yourself with others, you may spend your entire life trapped in a lonely cocoon of your own making."

"Kindness is seeing the good in others… and saying so."

"Tis the privilege of friendship to talk nonsense and to have your nonsense respected." (Charles Lamb)

"It's always someone who notices; someone who cares about your well-being, who recognizes that you have stopped trying and settled for less than your ability. You may want to listen to them."

"We are all travelers in the desert of life and the best we can find on our journey is an honest friend." (Robert Louis Stevenson)

"For me, nothing enlivens the soul like singing together in harmony."

Love & Friendship

"One person can make a difference but a group changes the world!"
(Mahatma Gandhi)

"There is none so rare, as the person who cares about others and regularly acts on that belief, without glory or any other prize in sight."

"Beware. There are those who camouflage their insincerity... behind a hearty laugh and a smile."

"Saying cruel or disrespectful things about others, behind their backs... is definitely not the best way of building trust."

Dave's LIFE LINES

"One side, alone, cannot fix a broken relationship… it can only delay the inevitable."

"If you like and get along with someone, then simply not having a lot in common with them… is probably a terrible reason to avoid being friends."

"An act of kindness is never wasted, whether the recipient is aware of it or not."

"Openly disliking a person is a sure way to become obsessed with hatred. Forgive, even if you can't forget… and learn to move on."

"Love and support your friends, but be careful not to lose yourself in the process."

"Try not to instantly select your best friends by the people you know with the most outgoing personalities. Speaking from experience, shy or quiet people just take a little more time and effort to get to know."

"True friendship does not require a person to always agree with their friends. Conversely, it encourages them to always speak honestly."

Dave's LIFE LINES

"A real friend is one who walks in when the rest of the world walks out." (Anon)

"Bad friendships age like a piece of stinky cheese."

"There is seldom a good reason to intentionally speak or act unkindly toward anyone. When you feel animosity toward someone, for whatever the reason, simply cool yourself down... and then calmly talk with them about it."

"You never really know what strangers are going through in their lives. So, every time you come across one, be sure to greet them with a smile... and always treat them kindly." (Anon)

"When a facial expression appears insincere, then so does its intended sentiment."

Dave's LIFE LINES

"If a friend asked me to lie for them, and I acquiesced their request, then we would no longer be friends… but accomplices in deceit."

"A conversation filled with laughter and fun is far more enjoyable than watching most of the movies out in theatres today!"

"A good friendship is not all smiles and laughter… but it always works hard to get you there."

"Many friendships from the past lie dormant due to inactivity… it's never too late to reawaken them."

"Simple disagreements with friends or family are a normal and benign activity. Save your energy and passion for those important battles, where winning or losing could truly make a meaningful difference in your life… or the lives of others, dear to you!"

"Be careful of speaking or acting too harshly to anyone, especially your young children, even in the name of love. Later, they may still feel the pain they believe you inflicted on them years earlier. Consequently, they may find it difficult, as adults, to ever have an honest relationship with you… even if you are both open to one."

"Being happy is not only about having fun with friends and family… but that certainly helps!"

"You will appreciate, tomorrow… that because you bit your tongue and counted to ten, you did NOT needlessly alienate your friends or family, by losing your temper and yelling at them, today."

"Often, when friends live apart, they grow apart. But true friends, will always share that special bond that was forged during those early years of their friendship… regardless of the time or distance separating them now."

"When we choose to be parents, we accept another human being as part of ourselves, and a large part of our emotional selves will stay with that person for as long as we live. From that time on, there will be another person on this earth whose orbit around us will affect us as surely as the moon affects the tides, and affect us in some ways more deeply than anyone else can. Our children are extensions of ourselves."
(Fred Rogers)

"You probably won't be close friends with everyone you meet, unless everyone you meet thinks a lot like you do, which in my experience… they don't!"

Dave's LIFE LINES

"A good friend is someone who thinks that you are a good egg even though he knows that you are slightly cracked." (Bernard Meltzer)

"True friendship is intimately knowing a person's weaknesses or flaws... but freely accepting them, as part of who they are."

"Although some of our dearest friends and family, for one reason or another, are not the ones we usually hang out with... they reside in our hearts, always."

"We love the things we love for what they are."
(Robert Frost)

"Jealousy is proof positive, you want something that someone else has... no matter how you spin it!"

"Trust is something that is hard to win, easy to lose… and never to be taken lightly." (Anon)

"If love is not at the center of your relationship… nothing on earth can hold it together for long."

"A good friend doesn't need to be asked for help… they just seem to know when you need it."

"Just because you haven't talked to someone for a very long time, does not necessarily mean that you still don't consider them to be friends."

"Sometimes… you are your own best friend."

"You may think that infatuation feels exactly like love, and in fact, it may... But it isn't. When an infatuation dies, everyone generally goes his or her own separate ways. But with love, when the tough times come, those in love... face them together."

"It is not a lack of love, but a lack of friendship that makes unhappy marriages." (Frederich Nietzsche)

"When you really want to help someone, try to make them feel empowered... not entitled."

"No friendship is perfect... accept and forgive."

Dave's LIFE LINES

"Everyone needs to know when their lives have gone seriously off-track. But they must also know… that it's never too late to fix it."

"Love is as gentle as a whisper, as caring as a soft smile and as meaningful as a warm embrace. There is nothing else like it in the entire world. When you find it… nurture it… and never let it go."

"When we think about those people we could least live without… those are the ones we love."

"Every time a person you care about is hurt... you hurt too. And every time that same person is gleeful... you share their happiness. Without a doubt, that's the personal connection that caring, always seems to build for us!"

"Sometimes, while talking to a friend, I grow so involved in the story I am telling, about a fun experience we had together, that when I finally finish speaking and surprisingly notice that my friend is wearing a very quizzical expression, I suddenly realize... wrong friend!"

"Every good friendship enriches your life... sometimes, forever."

Dave's LIFE LINES

"People are unreasonable, illogical and self-centered. Love them anyway." (Mother Teresa)

"The best way to make a friend, is to BE a friend."

"When you say something unduly harsh to people around you at work or at home, but later feel badly about it... Good!"

"Although you may not have the best history with someone, help them out, if you can, when they are in need. Nothing helps to mend a broken friendship... like friendship!"

"When a relationship goes sour, it's most common to point fingers and play the blame game, which is detrimental to both sides. Instead, why don't we just agree that the relationship is no longer working, and amicably part... but not as enemies?"

Dave's LIFE LINES

"Every good friendship should share about equal portions of give and take. Anything else, might mean that the friendship is in need of a tune-up."

"Nothing says that you and I have to agree on everything, in order to be friends. At times, an honest discussion, to air our differences, is called for... to make our friendship even stronger!"

"I have to admit that on a particularly difficult day, even a warm smile from a stranger, in passing, is enough to get my mind out of the doldrums and right back on track!"

"When I'm feeling down, I find that a timely and pleasant conversation with my friends or family members always brings my spirits right back up!"

"When someone I care about deeply, is taken from this world, although I will miss them, my memories will keep them alive and well in my heart... as long as I live."

"Don't strive to be adored... but loved!"

"As long as we're excited about something or someone in our lives... life is fun!"

Dave's LIFE LINES

"If you truly felt happy during a time in your past, there is no need to forget about it now, just because you may have experienced it long ago. Happiness is an unforgettable feeling that for some people, may be fleeting and so incredibly rare, giving us all the more reason to cherish and to remember it… every time it comes around."

"The fact that we can be so happy or so angry with those closest to us is proof positive that love can be an emotional roller coaster… But it's still love."

"When you like the people you are with… even house cleaning is fun!"

Love & Friendship

"It takes a lot more than being superficially nice to someone to build a lasting friendship. Know your friends from your acquaintances."

"You really know you're in love when you can't fall asleep because reality is finally better than your dreams." (Dr. Seuss)

Chapter Four:
ACHIEVEMENT!

Now we reach the part of this book dealing with personal achievement. Those achievements could cover anything from a change in your thinking to building the tallest skyscraper in the world! The following motivational thoughts, however, deal more with the mindset accompanying an achievement, and less with how to make a billion dollars. However, I do think that some of these thoughts could possibly help with that endeavor, as well!

"Creating solutions to problems is a lot more fun than dwelling on or losing sleep over them."

"When considering taking on a challenge, 'why,' is always the most important question to ask yourself before deciding."

"Maintaining a winning attitude and a fighting spirit are far more important than natural talent, when you're traveling the road to success."

"Never settle for the minimum accomplishment when you know that you can do better, even if that's all that's required of you. Greater achievement, always brings greater rewards."

"Not succeeding at something is no shame, but not even attempting it, when you really want to… is!"

"Don't settle for the best… make it WOW!"

"Whatever your heart finds to do... do it with all your might!"
(Ecclesiastes 9:10)

"Just as soon as we begin depending on ourselves to get things done... They do!"

"Keeping our hearts and minds focused on solving the greatest challenges in our lives... is how we eventually find the solutions."

"Although success seems to be mostly measured in monetary terms these days... I personally measure mine in happiness."

"Never allow a problem to become your worst nightmare. Instead, let the solution represent one of your greatest achievements."

"Don't be disillusioned. The road to success is often littered with failures and disappointments… every step of the way."

"A positive person hopes they can do it, while a motivated person always finds a way to get the job done!"

"There's no shame in it. Sometimes it just feels so right and completely necessary to stop what we are doing… and start all over again."

"While working on achieving something, the best way to help yourself overcome a mental block... is by helping someone else achieve the very same thing."

"Don't think that every achievement must be something spectacular, in order to be praise worthy. To a young child, something as simple as learning to tie their shoes, represents a monumental feat!"

"A glimmer of hope is a great thing to build on."

"If you don't believe you can succeed... you can't!"

"Nothing great was ever achieved without enthusiasm."
(Ralph Waldo Emerson)

"If you compete to win, but actually end up somewhere other than first place… Embrace the outcome. Learn from that experience and try again later!"

"Accomplish what you can, given your limitations, and then just for fun, challenge yourself… and defy those limitations!"

"In order to carry out a positive action, we must develop first, a positive vision." (Dalai Lama)

Dave's LIFE LINES

"One achievement usually leads to another."

"Start by doing what's necessary; then do what's possible; and suddenly you are doing the impossible!" *(St. Francis of Assisi)*

"Our achievements may be great, but it's actually the inexhaustible supply of effort and determination we somehow generated to get them done… that we will proudly remember for the rest of our lives!"

*"When it dawns upon you how fast time is passing by, don't regret all that you planned, but have not yet accomplished. Regrets lead to depression. Instead, adopt a positive mindset and look forward to all of those wonderful things you will surely accomplish in the future…
Then get to work!"*

"To the enlightened, even failures may be considered successes."

Dave's LIFE LINES

"The admirable trait of always doing your best is often a lonely road. But stay the course. You know it's the right thing to do… and maybe eventually… you will even inspire others around you to work harder."

"It's amazing how much can be achieved when we begin with a positive attitude, a smile and determination."

"Once you believe in your ability to succeed… you are already halfway there!"

"Make the road to your achievements fun!"

"Twenty years from now, you will be more disappointed by the things you didn't do… than by the things you did." (Mark Twain)

"Decide what you want to achieve… and then pursue it with a vengeance!"

"Positive thinking and a stubborn refusal to quit are always the keys to accomplishing the seemingly impossible."

"Perhaps people who don't enjoy much success… simply don't <u>believe</u> hard enough?"

"Our achievements will mean so much more... if we don't only accomplish them for ourselves."

"When you become excited about a personal project, never relinquish the entire responsibility of getting it done, to someone else. You will have far less to complain about at the end."

"When you see clearly in your mind what it is you want to accomplish and you work as hard as you can for it, only to ultimately fail... take solace in the fact that can always try again!"

"A success that is measured only by public approval... is a shallow one."

Achievement!

"When things aren't working out as planned… it's time to develop a better plan!"

"A ship in harbor is safe, but that is not what ships are built for."
(John A. Shedd)

Dave's LIFE LINES

"A great idea is nothing, unless you are inspired enough to create a plan for achieving it… and then doing so!"

"Nothing else in the world… not all the armies… is so powerful as an idea, whose time has come."
(Victor Hugo)

"One secret to a long and successful career, is the ability to reinvent yourself from time to time."

"I can't change the direction of the wind, but I can adjust my sails to always reach my destination."
(Jimmy Dean)

"Don't think. Thinking is the enemy of creativity. It's self-conscious and anything self-conscious is lousy. You can't 'try' to do things. You simply 'must' do things." (Ray Bradbury)

"If your achievements don't include a sense of pride, once you have completed them… then you probably could have done better!"

"A person who is self-driven to do their job well, may be tired and perhaps stressed, but down deep… I'll bet they are very happy!"

"There is nothing more frustrating than being a motivated person, working someplace... surrounded by unmotivated and lazy co-workers!"

"Isn't it curious that just as soon as we deal with one important task in our lives... another one immediately pops-up?"

"If you're not making mistakes, you're not trying hard enough!"
(Vince Lombardi)

"Being a good parent, a good friend or a good person, means that you are successful daily!"

"When we do something perfectly, in every respect, we should feel proud of that achievement? Right? So, why do we always seem to need someone else's approval first… before we can really feel good about it?"

"Living an 'exceptional life' does not necessarily mean that you are rich, powerful or celebrated… but it does mean that you are happy!"

"A toddler succeeds in small increments, while intermittently experiencing a lot of failures… before ultimately learning to walk."

Dave's LIFE LINES

"If you want to see the ocean, it's better for a man to travel the distance, than to wait for the ocean to come to him." (Anon)

"There are times when a waste of time… is not really a waste of time."

"I don't believe that the majority of people are born with less or more natural ability to succeed, than anyone else. Sometimes, personal handicaps or difficult situations actually create the 'driving force' for people to succeed! Some people, regardless of their situations, just seem to make better choices with what they are given, and work much harder at achieving their goals. We can all make ourselves into successful people... if we truly want to."

"Each time we achieve something important to us, we move just a little bit closer to becoming that accomplished person... we know we can be."

Dave's LIFE LINES

"The purposeful inactivity of your mind and body, robs you of all the exciting achievements and adventures, you 'would have had.'"

"Think positively, when considering a new project. Worrying too much about things that could go wrong… is the perfect recipe for never getting started."

"There are two thoughts, when it comes to becoming successful. The first, is to know somebody; but more importantly, the second… is to BECOME somebody."

"A creative man is motivated by the desire to achieve… not by the desire to beat others."
(Ayn Rand)

"Without leaps of imagination or dreaming, we lose the excitement of possibilities. Dreaming, after all, is a form of planning." (Gloria Steinem)

"Every chance we are offered in life is like a cookie. Either we embrace that opportunity, by eating it, or we ignore it, and watch that cookie grow stale and crumble away… before our very eyes."

*"We are not necessarily productive,
simply because we are busy...
But we are definitely BUSY,
when we are productive."*

*"Often times, those things that we
vehemently don't want to do... are the
very things that we should do!"*

*"Do not go where the path may lead,
go instead where there is no path...
and leave a trail."
(Ralph Waldo Emerson)*

*"While confidence garners respect...
desperation only garners pity."*

"Even if you are not the best songwriter, author, cook or painter in the world, there is still no greater sense of pride that you can get, than the thrill of creating something meaningful... from scratch!"

"Once you discover your purpose in life, good job! But just know that after that... is when the hard work and commitment really begins!"

"It is in your moments of decision that your destiny is shaped."
(Anthony Robbins)

"A mighty flame followeth a tiny spark." *(Dante)*

Dave's LIFE LINES

*"When making an important personal decision, if you find yourself concerned about how it will affect others, as well as yourself...
I'll bet you are loved!"*

"Never completely degrade your past, just because of a few failures. Every failure you experience, should be treated like valuable dust; first, learn from your failure, and then merely sweep it away... and begin again."

"The worth of your achievements should not be measured by what other people think... as much as by what you think."

Achievement!

"An opportunity is like an ice cream cone. It looks tempting, but if we wait too long to taste it… it will all melt away."

Dave's LIFE LINES

"To determine if you are more of a free thinker or a follower, ask yourself this simple question, 'How much of what I do… is really my idea?'"

"It really feels great when you dream of achieving something challenging and then later, you watch it all come true! There's usually a lot of hard work, of course, in getting there… But it's always well worth it!"

"An over-achiever is simply a go-getter… who happens to be addicted to success!"

*"Cheating to win is ultimately
not very satisfying."*

*"Working hard to achieve something
at a less than stellar level, because
you don't possess the necessary
skills to excel at it… is still an
achievement worthy of praise!"*

*"To succeed in life you need three
things: a wishbone, a backbone
and a funny bone."*
(Reba McEntire)

*"As a creative person, don't leave
even one thought unturned. Enjoy
being creative, and create!"*

Dave's LIFE LINES

"Any achievement you have that does not include the elements of hard work and determination, no matter how great... probably doesn't mean that much to you."

"Sometimes we become so absorbed in reaching a goal that it's hard for us to think of anything else! By comparison, actually <u>achieving that goal</u>, in this case, may sometimes feel like a bit of a letdown. But remember, it is still a worthy accomplishment!"

"Every little accomplishment should be acknowledged, but not necessarily celebrated... thus making our greatest accomplishments and related celebrations, more meaningful to us."

"Never allow yourself to fear failure so much that you refrain from pursuing any new ideas. After all, immediate monetary or social gratifications, are not the only gauges of determining success. If you are truly excited about a new idea, go it alone if you must… but pursue it!"

"Now is the time to begin achieving that dream, no matter how big or small. The duration of our lives is very uncertain… so the sooner the better."

"Our greatest achievement may be to divide our time to effectively cover every aspect of our lives!"

Dave's LIFE LINES

"Many people seem to believe that change for the sake of change is good. I'm all for progress, but I say, 'If it ain't broke, don't trash it'… just strive to improve it."

"Being grateful for everything you have is so important, but that should never stop you from also pursuing other things… if you choose to."

"Never dwell on the low points in your life, when things didn't seem capable of getting any worse. Instead, excitedly create new plans for your present and future… and then… go out and achieve them!"

Achievement!

"It took a while to figure this out, but being retired, at least for me, is the time to complete creative projects I may have begun some thirty years ago. It's not about making money, anymore… it's all about finally earning that sense of completion."

"Stand up to your obstacles and do something about them. You will find that they haven't half the strength you think they have."
(Norman Vincent Peale)

"When you agree to do something for somebody, never say, 'I'll try'… say and think, 'I will!'"

"We do not need to begin each day with a plan for what we expect to accomplish, but that does not mean that <u>nothing</u> will be achieved. There are always those days when a little spontaneity results in a far more exciting and productive outcome."

"Any accomplishment will only be as good as the 'clearly defined' or 'nebulous' goals set and achieved… as well as the intensity of effort used in achieving them!"

"Peaceful discussions and fact finding do a much better job of procuring the best solutions than angry and partisan posturing."

"Sometimes we get it in our heads that we must accomplish something that has no real worth or meaning to anybody else. But once we get it done... it really feels wonderful!"

"Have you ever noticed that successful people are often the ones who are initially unsuccessful? But rather than giving up, and becoming depressed, they continue to work hard, until they are finally successful? Let's hear it for tenacity!"

"Lord, grant that I may always desire more than I can accomplish."
(Michelangelo)

"Try not to rush through any potential achievements you decide to pursue. Take your time… and enjoy the process!"

Chapter Five:
RANDOM THOUGHTS!

In regards to this book, 'Random Thoughts,' are those motivational thoughts that speak the truth, but don't necessarily fit well into any one of my other four categories. These are amongst my favorite type of thoughts, because they are not limited by specific topics and, therefore, allow a writer the freedom to say exactly what it is they want to say!

"A day WITHOUT arguing politics, religion or sports is like a fun day at Disneyland without the high prices."

"The greatest weapon to neutralize the negative effects of bad luck… is your own sense of humor."

"Happiness is when what we think, do and say are all done in complete harmony." (Mahatma Gandhi)

*"When I thank God each morning for the new day, it reminds me that even with my problems...
I am still living a wonderful life!"*

"It has been proven, that a person's mind has enormous healing power over his or her body. I am pretty sure the instruction book is prayer."

"A good deed is only truly good, if the motives behind doing it... are not self-serving."

*"Just as soon as I realized how much I loved experiencing the exciting and emotional worlds created in my mind, through reading a good book...
I knew I had to become a writer!"*

"A lesson in life that I seem to relearn, over and over again, is that sometimes things will turn out a little bit differently than I'd expected. But often... it ends up being for the better."

"When you really think about it, hatred is the most useless and destructive thing in life, spawning nothing of value for anyone... only more hatred!"

"To me, the definition of a very satisfying career, is happily doing exactly what it is we want to do, surrounded by others of the same mindset... no matter what we find ourselves doing for a living!"

"The difference between good acting and sincerity... is found in the heart."

"The way to 'make things better,' always depends on whom you ask."

"A society of sheep must in time, beget a government of wolves."
(Bertrand de Jouvenel)

"Most people, I know, feel awkward going to a restaurant or event alone. I truly admire those people who don't need a companion to do the things they want to do, WHEN they choose to do them!"

"The preparation of a winner... is never finished."

"When I complete a task for someone in need, that I am in no way obligated to do, I understand what is important in life... just a little bit better."

"Popularity is overrated. Sometimes it's more fun to be invisible."

"If there were no mirrors, people would probably not be as caught up with HOW they looked, so instead, they could concentrate more of their energy on WHO they were!"

"Creating drama is best suited for the stage."

"A man who tells you he will do something, but does not… is a polite liar." (Aesop)

"No matter where you go, you've never really left."

"If 'crazy freeway driving' was an Olympic sport, all the winners would surely be from California!"

"When you find yourself feeling frustrated, trying to achieve something, with little or no success, it's time to move on to something you are already good at, in order to feel confident again. There will always be plenty of time to feel frustrated again tomorrow!"

"When determining the most important goals to pursue in life, place 'knowing yourself,' first!"

*"Just because a person occupies a high position, does not guarantee that they are unbiased, honest or well-qualified. The good news is...
it usually doesn't take us
very long to figure it out!"*

*"No one has the right to consume happiness without producing it."
(Helen Keller)*

*"Flowers, like people, are most beautiful, once you get
past their thorns."*

"Thank God, every morning for giving you another day of life... and then do something good with it!"

"Happiness is about balance. Never rely solely on other people to make you happy. Find your own happiness and share it freely with others, as they have shared theirs with you. As a result, with each of you giving freely... the happiness will truly be in balance!"

"Arrogance is curdled confidence... turned obnoxious."

"In time, everything old is new again. It's all about the packaging!"

"The older you get, the smarter you get... You hope, anyway!"

"Unfortunately, we cannot just call upon inspiration, any time we want it. True inspiration, chooses to unveil itself to us very calmly and quietly... Most unexpectedly."

"If anyone ever brazenly accuses you of 'only talking to hear the sound of your own voice,' next time you speak to them, just for fun, smile... and use someone else's voice."

"The difference between stupidity and genius is that genius has its limits." (Albert Einstein)

"Music can calm the soul, or send it soaring!"

"Imagine that we were all plants and the beauty of our flowers was completely dependent upon how kindly we treated the other plants. How beautiful do you think your flowers would be?"

"Angry people should not send emails!"

Dave's LIFE LINES

"The most pathetic person in the world is someone who has sight… but has no vision." (Helen Keller)

"Old age is like everything else. To make a success of it, you've got to start young." (Fred Astaire)

"It's not our problems that make us crazy… but our bad reactions to them."

"Once proved to be a liar or a cheat, it is very difficult to ever regain people's trust again."

*"If it makes you laugh, and it's not
intentionally hurting anyone,
there is nothing innately wrong
with your sense of humor... even if
you're the only one who gets it."*

*"I treasure my alone time. That's
the only time when I feel
completely like myself."*

*"Life without creativity is colorless...
always painted in black and white."*

*"Happiness was never meant for one
person to hoard... it has always
been meant to be shared."*

"There are two kinds of light; the glow that illuminates, and the glare that obscures."
(James Thurber)

"If you feel that you are different than a lot of other people around you, then congratulations! You are! Celebrate your originality!"

"The two coolest things about the imagination are one, how our ability to create new ideas seems to be endless and two, how there are no right or wrong ideas, only the question of relevance; if it's the best idea for what we are currently working on."

"Iron rusts from disuse; stagnant water loses its purity and in cold weather becomes frozen; even so does inaction sap the vigor of the mind."
(Leonardo da Vinci)

"If you are not making everything you do, better, and everyone you care about, happier? Then what exactly ARE you doing?"

"Never rely on a lengthy list of achievements to define how successful your life has been. Simply ask yourself, 'How happy am I?'"

"To disrespect someone… invites others to disrespect you."

"As a well spent day brings happy sleep, so a well spent life brings happy death." (Leonardo da Vinci)

"Simultaneously, each of us lives in two different realms; the first, is the world around us, while the second, is the world inside our heads. In order to be truly happy, one of our most diligent jobs in life must be to successfully make the one realm… compatible with the other."

"A man is not honest, simply because he's never had the chance to steal!" (Russian proverb)

"You'll never find a rainbow if you're looking down." (Charles Chaplin)

"When you have eliminated the impossible, that which remains, however improbable, must be the truth!" (Sir Arthur Conan Doyle)

"Leadership is often confused with popularity and idolizing. But the best leaders… are more concerned with their inherent job descriptions."

"Change is serious stuff. People who experience it… are never the same again!"

"Never gauge how good your life is by its lack of inherent challenges or problems. Often, conquering those very challenges or solving those problems... is the very thing that makes your life feel so meaningful."

"Why is everyone so sensitive these days? Get over it, stupid!" (Anon)

"Unforced change, is a healthy part of life."

"You should never dwell on the past... unless you're writing a book about it."

"Your life can be as full as you make it… but it can also be as empty."

"When I am working on a problem, I never think about beauty… but when I have finished, if the solution is not beautiful, I know it is wrong."
(R. Buckminster Fuller)

"When I was younger, I could remember anything… whether it happened or not." (Mark Twain)

"When you forgive, you in no way change the past… but you sure do change the future."
(Bernard Meltzer)

Dave's LIFE LINES

*"A talented and successful ass…
is still an ass!"
(Rodney Dangerfield)*

*"The world is full of willing people;
some willing to work… the rest
willing to let them." (Robert Frost)*

"The toughest challenges, for any person to take on, do not deal with world peace, a cure for cancer or climate change... they deal with conquering their own inherent weaknesses."

"The moment you realize that life is a never-ending plethora of incredible opportunities... is the moment when you really start living."

"One of the most reliable truths in regards to having a happy life, is understanding that we plan for the future and remember the past... but we live for today."

Dave's LIFE LINES

"You always know that it's going to be a great day, when you have nowhere to be, you are still dressed in your jammies at noon and it feels like anything is possible!"

"If we have a fight and later, after making up, we can't agree on whose fault it was? Let's just agree that it's San Andreas' Fault!" (Anon)

"It doesn't matter how old you are. You are never too old to have your feelings hurt!"

"Many people like to be part of a group, but I prefer to work alone. That way, I'm always in charge!"

"Good judgment comes from experience, and experience usually comes... from bad judgment." (Anon)

"Nature inspires like nothing else."

"In order for three people to keep a secret... two must be dead." (Benjamin Franklin)

"Don't be afraid of anything or anyone... But respect them all."

"Even on a tough day, there is always something positive to remember."

Dave's LIFE LINES

*"Never reach a conclusion about anything that's based solely on another person's opinion.
One man's trash is another man's treasure!"*

"To the motivated... every moment is exciting!"

*"Although many things I have experienced in life are wonderful and exciting, nothing can compare with the awe I felt when watching our baby boy, share his first smile with me!
It was magical!"*

"If your behavior is being dictated by the fear of breaking a rule and getting in trouble… then you have yet to take charge of your own life."

"There are three types of people in the world; those who tear it down, those who do nothing for it… and those who build it up. People will know, by your actions… which one of them you are."

"Dreaming is that special fantasy world we enter each night, where we can experience adventure, fright, romance, the bizarre or humorous, in the safety of our own beds and it never costs us a cent!"

Dave's LIFE LINES

"Everyone's life, no matter how difficult, is a gift and an opportunity. What we do with it every day, will undoubtedly... define us."

"You can appreciate what a person says, and the obvious sincerity behind it... but still disagree."

"Be wary of people with secret agendas."

"Don't spend too much time trying to figure out what makes the Earth and sky so beautiful... just say, 'thank you,' and enjoy the view."

"If you are outstanding at trying to be a good person, you may not get the adulation of a rock star or a popular actor... but you will get something much better... the love, trust and respect of those who know and depend upon you."

"My secret to always feeling vital and alive is to never be without a creative project. As long as they are not finished... neither am I!"

"To avoid criticism, do nothing, say nothing and be nothing!"
(Elbert Hubbard)

"Sometimes, although we probably don't intend to, during the most inopportune moments... we fart!"

"When we appreciate the heartfelt determination and creativity demonstrated by folks around us, we can't help but become inspired!"

"Although some people incessantly dwell on who they used to be, a far more important question to answer, is... who are you NOW?"

"To fault a person for their beliefs implies that your beliefs are better. How do you know?"

"Strive to be the real you, whenever possible. Unless, of course, you are an actor, a spy, a salesman, a politician, a criminal or a compulsive liar... in which case, your job descriptions may often require you to be someone else."

"Never have the gall to demand the best from others... unless you are demanding the same from yourself!"

"Don't try to avoid problems; they have a way of always finding you no matter what you do! Instead, armed with a positive attitude, calmly deal with them. Then your life, along with the lives of your loved ones... will be a whole lot happier."

Dave's LIFE LINES

"There are those folks who are always spontaneously full of exciting ideas and super energy, yet may also seem to be scatterbrained and hyperactive. Those are truly my kind of people!"

"My belief has always been that ill-tempered people are actually really nice folks… who have been plagued by a permanent migraine headache!"

"Sunrise, Sunset. Ah! But what is it we do with all of the hours in-between, that is worthy of such glorious beauty? You decide… The possibilities are endless."

"A good laugh and a long sleep are the two best cures for anything."
(Irish proverb)

"Doing something, always beats doing nothing!"

"If someone you know is suddenly rude to you, for no apparent reason... trust me, there's a reason!"

"Anyone who looks for problems... is certain to find them."

"When we have planned and arranged for an exciting trip in the near future, we have almost as much fun dreaming about it... as we do going on the trip, itself!"

"We cannot recapture the past, but we can certainly use the best parts as a starting point for the future."

"The constant stream of negative political rhetoric aired on some television and radio shows, only becomes unbearable... if we choose to listen to it."

"When we take the time to show our appreciation to others for their exceptional achievements... we encourage them to do it again."

"In order to stop dreading any approaching social obligations, you should think of reasons you could actually look forward to attending them and then do exactly that! Your obligations won't change, of course, but you will sure save a lot of precious time by not worrying about them!"

"Happiness is mostly a team sport."

"The young always have the same problem... how to rebel and conform at the same time. They have solved this by defying their parents and copying one another."
(Quentin Crisp)

"Changing your mind is not a sign of weakness, it's a sign of... changing your mind."

"Clothes make the man. Naked people have little or no influence on society." (Mark Twain)

"A halo has to fall only a few inches to become a noose." (Anon)

*"When we appreciate the beautiful world around us, as well as how blessed our lives really are...
Who has a reason to complain?"*

"There are dark shadows on the earth, but its lights are stronger in the contrast." (Charles Dickens)

"A person who insults you with a gentle voice and a warm smile is equally as insulting as a person who insults you through an angry tirade... although it almost feels worse?"

"Don't compare your skills with someone else's simply to determine which of you is more talented. Instead, work together to create something of value... which neither of you could have ever created by yourselves!"

"One of the sanest, surest, and most generous joys of life, comes from being happy over the good fortune of others." (Robert A. Heinlein)

"There is always something new to see in the unchanging night sky." (Fritz Leiber)

"Manners help people learn to be more conscientious. I like that."

"An encouraging smile and a hug on a bad day… do more for reviving our spirits than one hundred ice cream cones!"

"To me, retirement is the time when I am finally allowed to completely think, act and speak, like myself! Uh oh!"

"All that we see or seem is but a dream within a dream."
(Edgar Allan Poe)

"Although it's clear that manners have all but become extinct for many people, I still enjoy saying and hearing, 'thank you,' or 'excuse me,' when the situation presents itself."

"We are what we think. All that we are arises with our thoughts. With our thoughts, we make the world."
(Buddha)

"Believing in peace, harmony and goodness… only seems silly to those who don't!"

"Good things happen… to those who are good."

*"Anyone can share their
own words of wisdom...*

*But proving them true
may be hard?*

*The author must swear
ev'ry word's bona fide...*

*Or found in a store's
Hallmark card!"
(Anon)*

*"We don't always know how other
people feel about us, but we shouldn't
be overly concerned. If we are acting
with kindness, honesty, and without
grudges, then how others view us...
should be of little consequence
and entirely up to them."*

Dave's LIFE LINES

"Singing is a well-known therapy for alleviating stress and anxiety and as it turns out… it doesn't even matter if you sing in tune!"

"Fish and visitors stink in 3 days."
(Ben Franklin)

"Any group activity that people willingly join into, where everyone enjoys doing it equally well (with no hangovers) and where everyone feels better at the end of it than at the beginning… must involve group singing!"

"The fact that each of us is different, means that we are all like puzzle pieces, going through life trying to figure out where we best fit in. But as soon as that answer becomes clear… Our adventure truly begins in earnest!"

"Life is a great maze that everyone must successfully learn to navigate."

"It seems as though some people need to be fighting someone or something all of the time, in order to give their lives more meaning. I don't."

"Never place your personal opinion ahead of making the best decision, unless by chance... they are one and the same!"

"You can't depend on your eyes when your imagination is out of focus."
(Mark Twain)

"The weather should not have the power to dictate a person's mood... unless that mood is happy!"

"Some people become so comfortable as followers, that they never once consider pursuing their potential as leaders."

"It's fine to admire or even to emulate another person you look up to. But never feel the need to BE that person. Instead… be you, inspired by them."

"Life and love are the two things that we must cherish above all else. They are gifts from God."

"Happiness is one part desire, one part determination, one part luck… and seven parts love!"

"I used to believe that praying for people or silently wishing them well, could somehow help them... and I still do."

"You can't really fake charisma or wit. But a whole lot of people sure do make fools out of themselves trying!"

"It's funny how some of the bad behaviors we were taught in school and church to avoid doing, such as name calling and bullying... are the very behaviors many politicians use on a daily basis? Can anyone say, double standard?"

"Many people spend their lives searching for answers, never once realizing… that it's probably much quicker to create them!"

"Every problem should only be viewed as a diversion in our lives… hindering us at times, but never being ultimately allowed to defeat us."

"Shyness is flair, that just takes longer to share."

"The saying, 'blood is thicker than water,' although originally written about family and friends… is actually better suited to vampires."

Dave's LIFE LINES

Just because you get older, your dreams are still fresh as ever. Have faith that if you continue to believe in them... it's just a matter of time."

"He who knows his own strengths, talents and skills and flawlessly exercises them daily, is undoubtedly ready for the challenge... of learning something new."

"Following every perceived failure, comes rebirth, growth and the opportunity for success... if we just stick around long enough without giving up!"

"Regardless of who you are, nothing absolves you from choosing not to do the right thing, even when 'doing the right thing' goes counter to what you feel is best for you."

"I feel very sorry for those people without well developed or active imaginations. They miss out on all of those magical thoughts... and the fun that results from them!"

"Anyone who believes in shutting out and condemning any ideas that differ from their own... has forgotten why America was founded."

Dave's LIFE LINES

*"To be a good loser…
is to learn how to win."
(Carl Sandburg)*

"Just a dash of imagination can make the most mundane activity fun."

"Nobody's perfect but no one is beyond remorse and redemption, either… no matter how hard they may try!"

"On a day when you feel 'lost,' get excited about doing something fun, anything, especially if it involves other people… and then actually do it! Like magic, you will happily 'find yourself,' once again!"

"An opinionated person may not be the most popular being in the room, but they'll never be bored, judging and spawning negative opinions about every face they see and then arrogantly sharing them with the rumormongers and anyone else who will listen."

"There's a way to do it better. Find it!" (Thomas Edison)

"If your job has more pressure in it than you can comfortably handle, then starting a new job, that makes you happier, is a perfect alternative to being miserable... even if it involves a pay cut."

Dave's LIFE LINES

"When someone who perceives you as being weaker and less powerful than they are, tries to bully you from time to time… calmly stand up for yourself. Never bow to bullies!"

"Christmas waves a magic wand over this world, and behold, everything is softer and more beautiful."
(Norman Vincent Peale)

"When elected leaders continually force unpopular changes on their people, causing antagonism to develop… it's definitely time for a new election."

"Living presents each of us with an amazing opportunity to create the perfect life! It's only to those unfortunate souls who cease caring about anything… that life may ultimately seem pointless and void."

"The fact that people tell me there is no such thing as a unicorn… does not mean that there is not one living in my imagination, right now!"

"Just because you trained for a certain vocation, does not mean that you and the job are necessarily a good match? Stay open minded. You'll know when you've found that 'perfect job.'"

"We don't always appreciate how much someone has inspired us, until years later, when we finally find the time to think about it and to vividly see the fruits of their impact upon our lives… and through us, their impact upon others."

"Money, cars and a house do not make a marriage complete, but they do complement it perfectly!"

"It's a lot easier to excel if you are naturally talented at something. But, if you're not, years of professional training will certainly make you better. However, it's your level of determination, which will ultimately decide… HOW MUCH BETTER."

"When seeking closure to an argument… compromise always works better than stubbornness."

"In spite of the fact that 'majority rules,' and although I do honor that premise, I reserve the right to maintain my differing points of view, whenever I'm in the minority… even if I'm there alone."

"If people spent as much time respecting others as they do complaining about them, the world would sure be a happier place."

"Pursuing a project that you simply want to do… needs no better reason!"

Dave's LIFE LINES

"I admire most people for one reason or another. But I especially admire people who are hard workers, honest, sincere, witty and kind. They are the coolest people I know!"

"Each of our lives is so precious, not only to us, but to our friends and family who love having us around. As long as we are alive, it's never too late to make our lives, as well as the lives of others, better and more fulfilling. Ready, set, go!"

Illustrations

1. *I Believe In Santa Claus......6*
2. *Creativity Is Intelligence......11*
3. *If We Were Meant To Be........16*
4. *People Who Don't Believe......21*
5. *Sometimes The Key..............36*
6. *Self-Reflection....................43*
7. *There Is No Outside Cure......51*
8. *Be Careful That You Practice..59*
9. *Until You Begin Sharing.........71*
10. *Bad Friendships Age............76*
11. *A Good Friend Is Someone....82*
12. *People Are Unreasonable......88*
13. *One Achievement Always.......100*
14. *When Things Aren't..............105*
15. *If You Want To See...............110*
16. *An Opportunity Is Like..........117*
17. *Imagine That We.................137*
18. *A Talented And Successful.....146*
19. *Those Folks Who Are...........156*
20. *Singing Is A Well-Known.......166*

www.ingramcontent.com/pod-product-compliance
Lightning Source LLC
Chambersburg PA
CBHW022105040426
42451CB00007B/132